Counting the Continents

Ellen K. Mitten

ROURKE PUBLISHING

Vero Beach, Florida 32964

www.rourkepublishing.com

PHOTO CREDITS: © Jani Bryson: Title Page, 23; © Jan Rysavy: 3, 22, 23; © bonnie jacobs: 5; © ziggymaj: all maps, 22; © iofoto: 7; © best photo: 9; © Ian Cumberland: 9, 13, 15; © Graeme Purdy: 11; © Samuel Clarke: 13; © Anastasiya Rutkovskaya: 15; © sdewdney: 17; © Jan Will: 17 © Thomas Perkins: 19; © asiseeit: 21, 23; © Robert Bremec: 22

Edited by Meg Greve

Cover design by Nicola Stratford bppublishing.com
Interior design by Tara Raymo

Library of Congress Cataloging-in-Publication Data

Mitten, Ellen.
  Counting the continents / Ellen K. Mitten.
    p. cm. -- (Little world geography)
  ISBN 978-1-60694-422-6 (hard cover)
  ISBN 978-1-60694-538-4 (soft cover)
  ISBN 978-1-60694-589-6 (bilingual)
  1. Continents--Juvenile literature. I. Title.
  G133.M55 2009
  910.914'1--dc22
                            2009005744

Rourke Publishing
Printed in the United States of America, North Mankato, Minnesota
051110
051110LP-B

www.rourkepublishing.com - rourke@rourkepublishing.com
Post Office Box 643328 Vero Beach, Florida 32964

The **Earth** is made up of **land** and water.

We call the largest areas of land on Earth **continents**.

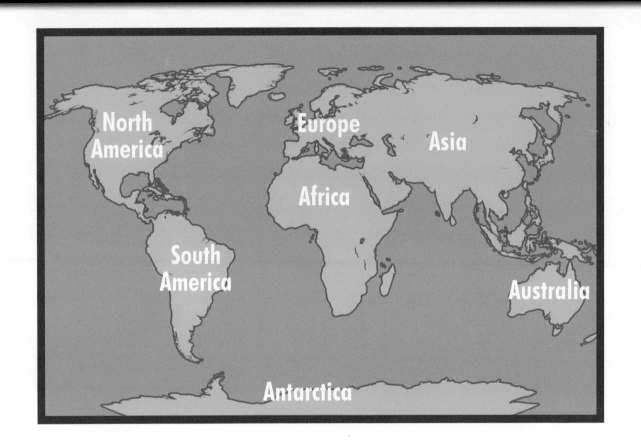

Let's count the continents!

Arctic Ocean

Beaufort Sea

Baffin Bay

Greenland Sea

Kara Sea

Laptev

Barents Sea

Arctic Circle

Norwegian Sea

Hudson Bay

Labrador Sea

North Sea

Gulf of Alaska

NORTH AMERICA

ASIA

rth ific ean

North Atlantic Ocean

AFRICA

Cancer

Gulf

0   650   1,300 Miles
0   650   1,300 KM

AM

an O

Capricorn

Prime Meridian

h Pacific Ocean

Antarctic Ci

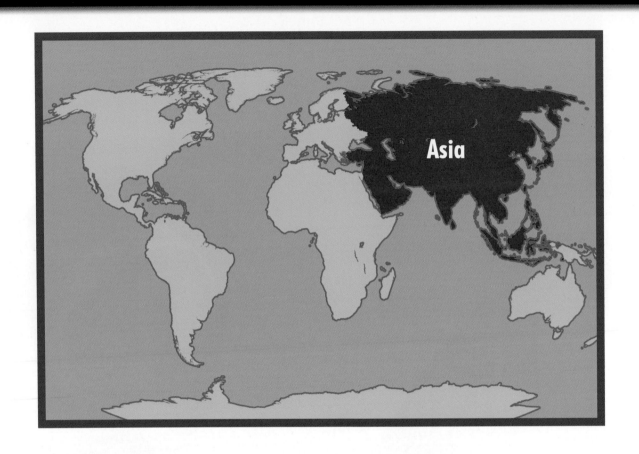

Asia is the largest continent.
Can you find it?

The Great Wall of China was built in Asia about 2,200 years ago!

Africa is the second largest continent. Which one is it?

Africa is home to the cheetah, the world's fastest animal.

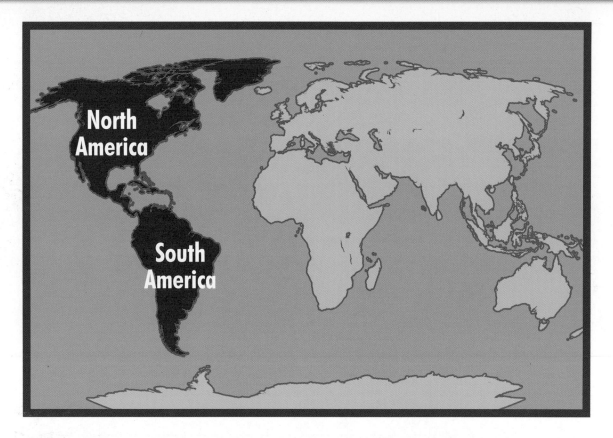

North America and South America are connected. Where are they?

South America is home to the largest rain forest in the world.

13

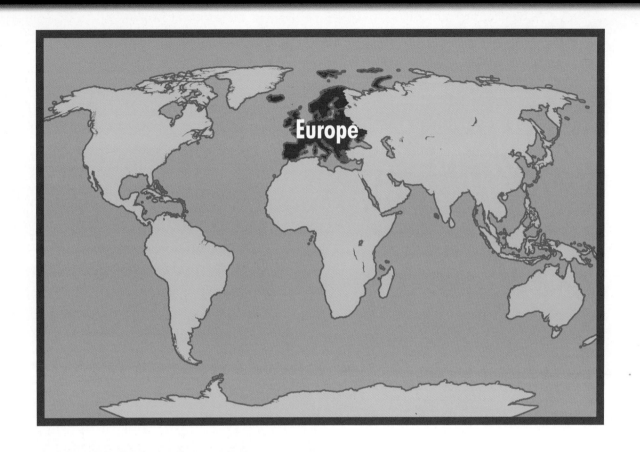

Europe is the only continent without a **desert**. Where is it?

The Ural Mountains separate Europe and Asia.

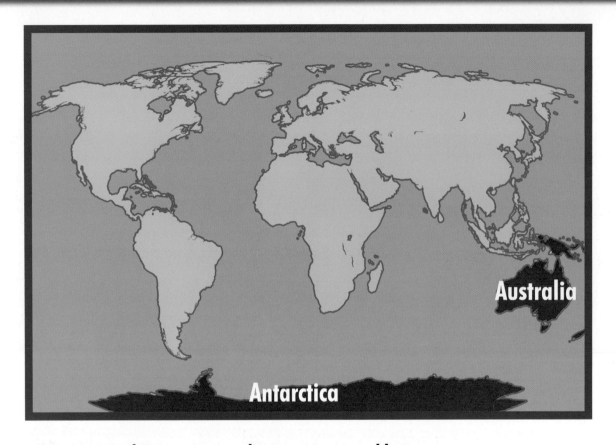

Australia is the smallest continent. Antarctica is the coldest. Where are they?

Australia is home to the kangaroo. Antarctica is home to the Emperor penguin.

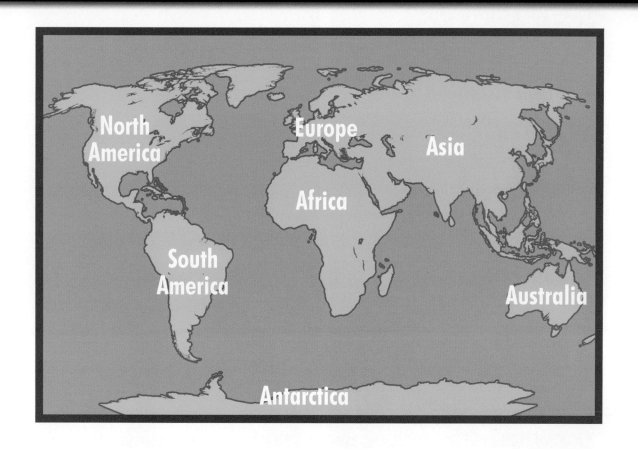

How many continents are there?

Spin a **globe** or open a **map,**
count the seven continents!

GLOSSARY

 **continents** (KON-tuh-nuhnts): The largest land masses on Earth. They are Asia, Africa, Europe, North America, South America, Australia, and Antarctica.

 **desert** (DEZ-urt): A large, dry area of land that gets very little rain and is sandy. Very few plants can grow because there is not enough water.

 **Earth** (URTH): The planet on which we live. Earth is the third planet from the Sun, between Venus and Mars.